LET'S LOOK AT A MASTERPIECE

LET'S LOOK AT A MASTERPIECE

Classic Art to Cherish with a Child

Madeleine Stebbins

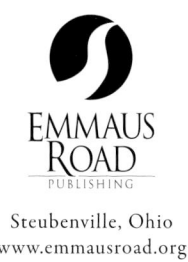

Steubenville, Ohio
www.emmausroad.org

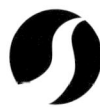

Emmaus Road Publishing
1468 Parkview Circle
Steubenville, Ohio 43952

©2018 Madeleine Stebbins
All rights reserved. Published 2018
Printed in the United States of America

Library of Congress Cataloging-in-Publication Data
Names: Stebbins, Madeleine, author.
Title: Let's look at a masterpiece : classic art to cherish with a child / Madeleine Stebbins.
Description: Steubenville, Ohio : Emmaus Road, [2018] | Audience: Grade K-3
Identifiers: LCCN 2018040563| ISBN 9781949013092 (hard cover) | ISBN 9781949013108 (pbk.)
Subjects: LCSH: Spirituality in art--Juvenile literature. | Christian art and symbolism--Juvenile literature.
Classification: LCC N8248.S77 S735 2018 | DDC 704.9/482--dc23 LC record available at https://lccn.loc.gov/2018040563

Unless otherwise noted, Scripture quotations are taken from The Revised Standard Version Second Catholic Edition (Ignatius Edition) Copyright © 2006 by the Division of Christian Education of the National Council of the Churches of Christ in the United States of America. Used by permission. All rights reserved.

Excerpts from the Catechism of the Catholic Church, second edition, copyright © 2000, Libreria Editrice Vaticana--United States Conference of Catholic Bishops, Washington, D.C.

Front cover image: *Adoration of the Magi (ca. 1440–60)* by Fra Angelico and Fra Filippo Lippi, National Gallery of Art, Washington DC, United States

Cover design and layout by Margaret Ryland

*To each child looking at and reading this book.
May it bring joy to your heart.*

*"Unless you turn and become like children,
you will never enter the kingdom of heaven."
—Matthew 18:3*

The Annunciation (c. 1482)
Hans Memling (c. 1430–1494) / Metropolitan Museum of Art, New York, United States

The Angel's Message

THE BLESSED VIRGIN is alone when suddenly the Archangel Gabriel appears to her. He says to Mary, "Hail, full of grace. The Lord is with thee." He tells her she will be the mother of Jesus, the Son of God.

Mary wonders and is so amazed that in this picture she is almost fainting. Angels come to hold her up and treat her like a princess.

But Gabriel tells her, "Fear not.... The Holy Spirit will come over you." Do you see the dove? It is the Holy Spirit.

Gabriel wears the vestments of a priest because his words are sacred and heavenly.

The lily on the right symbolizes Mary's purity.

Mary, the handmaid of the Lord, has one hand humbly on her breast. Her other hand is on the Bible, because she understands that this message is wonderful.

This is the extraordinary moment when God becomes flesh, one of us. It is a great mystery.

> "The child to be born will be called holy, the Son of God.... of His Kingdom there will be no end."
>
> —LUKE 1:35, 33

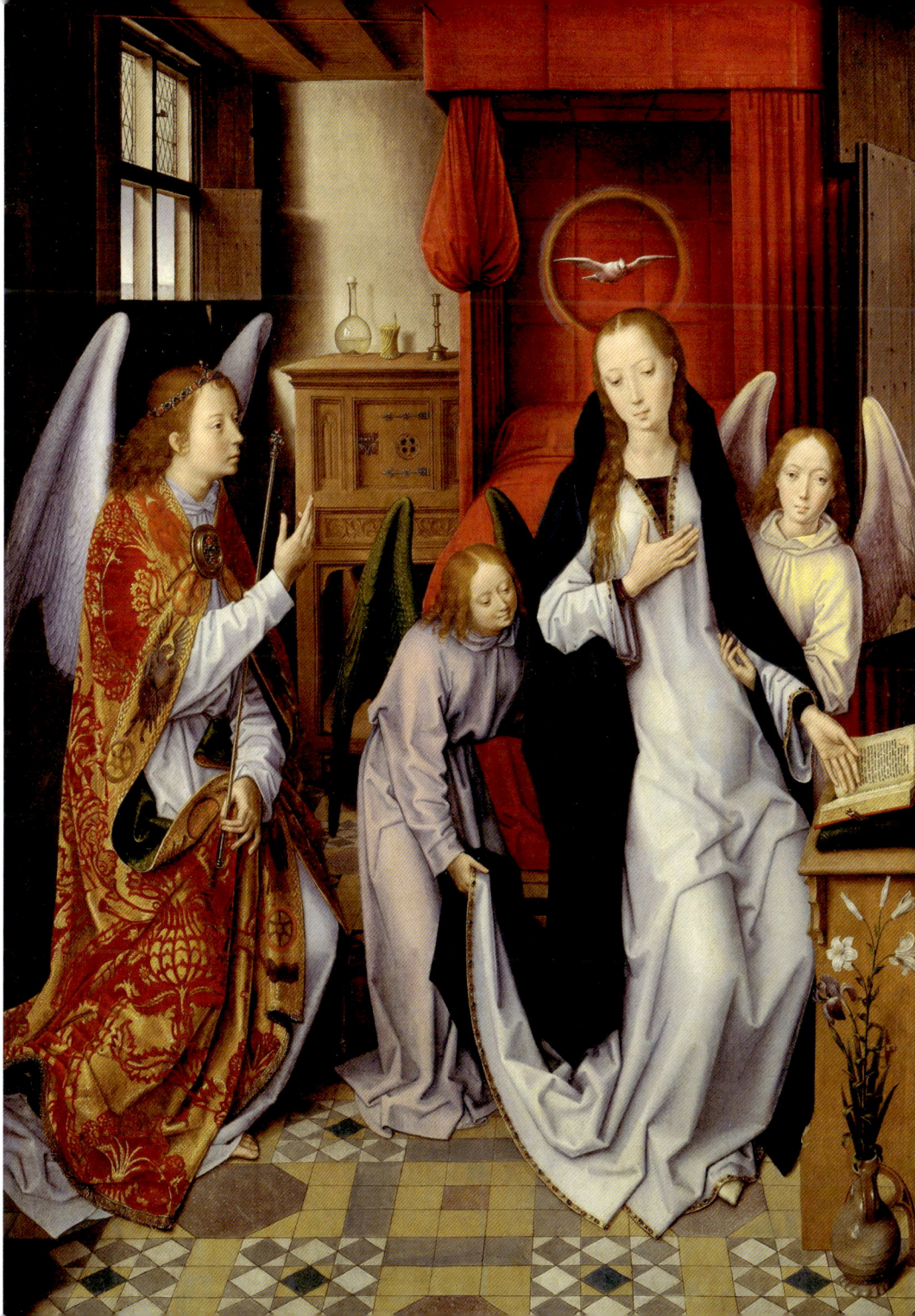

The Visitation (1306)
Giotto di Bondone (1266/7–1337) / Scrovegni Chapel, Padua, Italy

Joy and Expectation

After the Blessed Virgin Mary found out that she would be the mother of God, and the Child was in her womb, she ran to tell her cousin Elizabeth.

Elizabeth was also expecting a baby. Who was that baby?

He would be John the Baptist.

When the two women met, the baby inside Elizabeth jumped for joy! In this miraculous way, the baby greeted Jesus. And Elizabeth suddenly understood that it was the Lord inside Mary, who was now the mother of God.

Elizabeth cried out, "Blessed art thou among women, and blessed is the fruit of thy womb!"

Mary would say a great prayer of praise and thanksgiving for this marvelous mystery.

We see her here as a queen. At the same time, she is humble; not glorifying herself, but giving God the glory.

Elizabeth looks up to Mary and honors her. They love each other and want to serve each other.

Their hearts are filled with a deep joy.

> "My soul magnifies the Lord,
> And my spirit rejoices in God my Savior..."
>
> —Luke 1:46–47

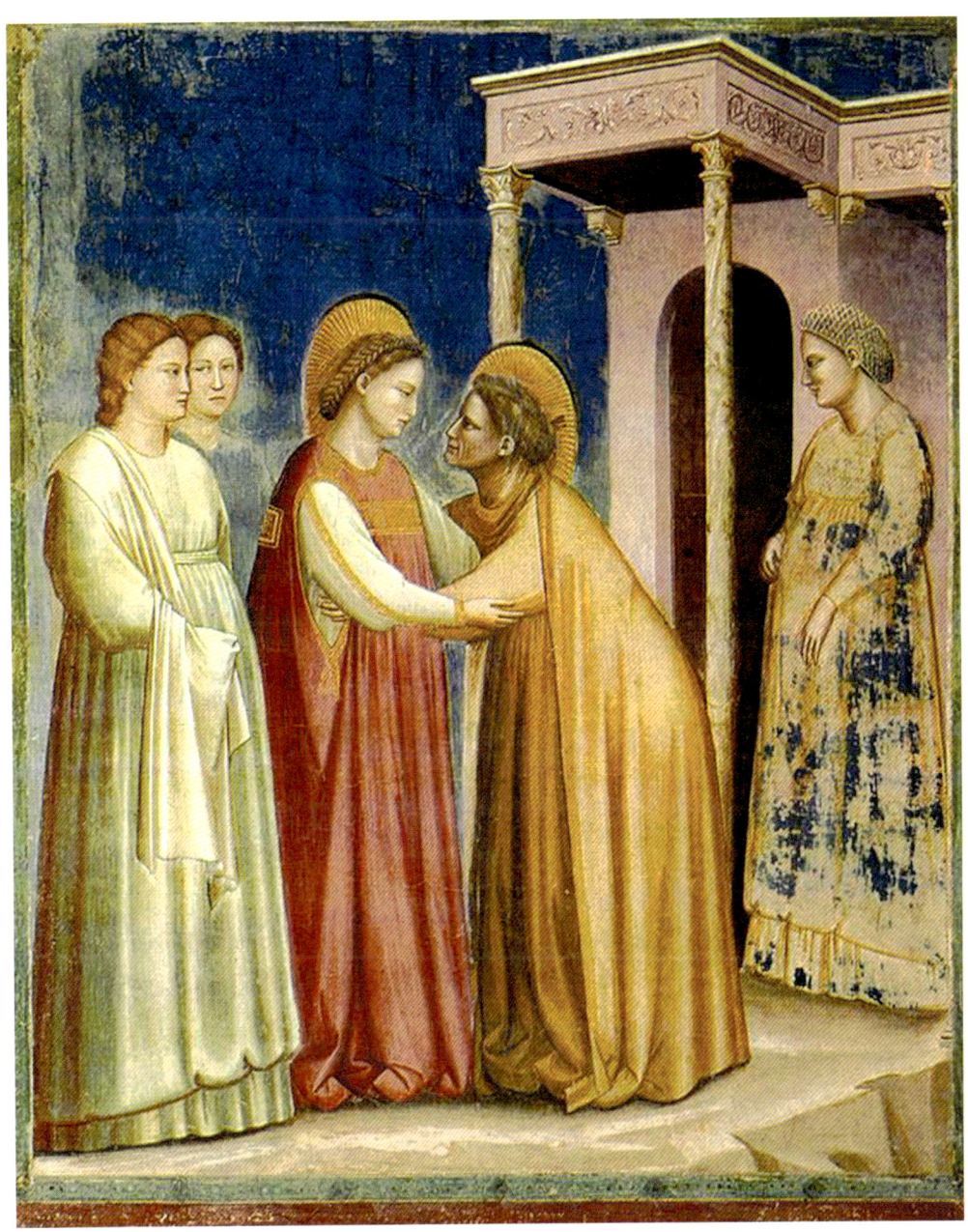

The Adoration of the Magi (1440, 1460)
Fra Angelico (c. 1395–1455), completed by Filippo Lippi (1406–1469) /
National Gallery of Art, Washington, DC, United States

His Glory Fills the Earth

AFTER THE ANGELS appeared to the shepherds to tell them the great news of the birth of the Messiah, Jesus, many people heard about it. This picture shows that after the Magi (or three kings) followed the star, large crowds started coming.

Here we see streams of people from every nation wanting to adore the Child. They are so excited that they run full of exultation and joy in colorful clothes.

The three kings in front are bringing gifts and kneeling in reverent adoration before this little King. One of them is kissing His foot.

Jesus is sitting on His mother's lap. She bends over her Child with tender love, with Joseph next to her.

We see Jerusalem like a bit of heaven on the top of the hill on the right.

Do you see the beautiful peacock? It is a symbol of immortality, which means that Jesus brings life that never ends.

> "The glory of the LORD has risen upon you. . . .
> And nations shall walk by your light,
> And kings in the brightness of your rising.
> . . . your heart shall thrill and rejoice."
>
> —ISAIAH 60:1, 3, 5

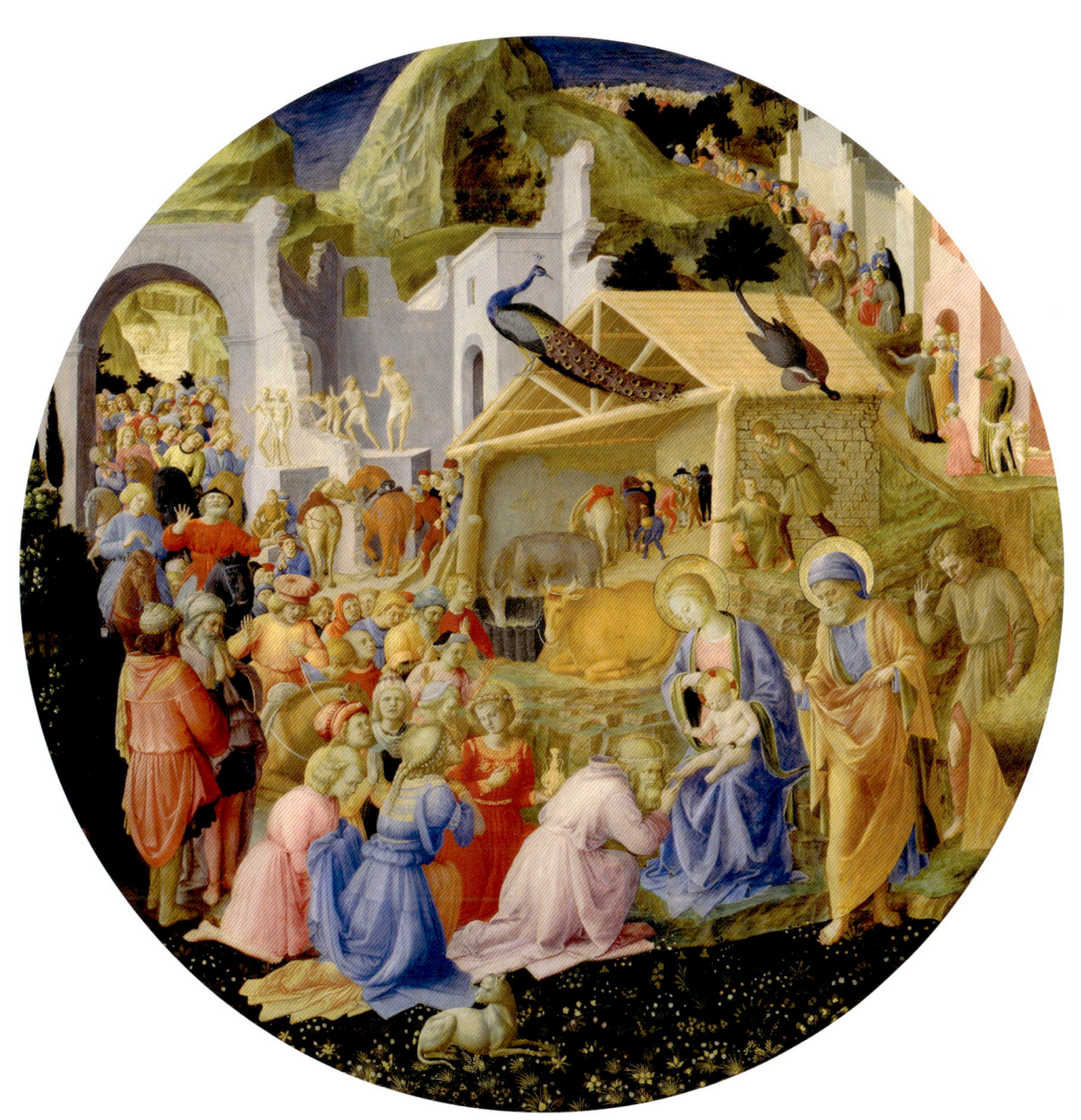

Simeon with the Christ Child in the Temple (1669)
Rembrandt Harmenszoon van Rijn (c. 1606–1669) / National Museum, Stockholm, Sweden

Simeon and Anna's Long-Awaited Savior

MARY AND JOSEPH brought the infant Jesus to present Him in the Temple, according to the Jewish custom.

The Holy Spirit told an old devout Jewish man named Simeon that he would not die before he had seen the Messiah, that is, the Savior: Jesus Christ.

Here an elderly woman, Anna, is with Simeon.

When Simeon took Jesus in his arms, he was suddenly inspired by the Holy Spirit, who came like a light shining over his head.

Simeon then recognized that here was the Savior of the World, who would be a light to all nations and the glory of Israel.

He was awestruck. It was as if he saw a vision when his eyes were closed; he experienced a foretaste of heaven. Simeon's lips opened in prophecy. He said to God, "Now dismiss your servant in peace, because my eyes have seen your salvation."

He also prophesied that a sword would pierce Mary's heart.

"A light for revelation to the Gentiles, and glory to your people Israel."

—LUKE 2:32

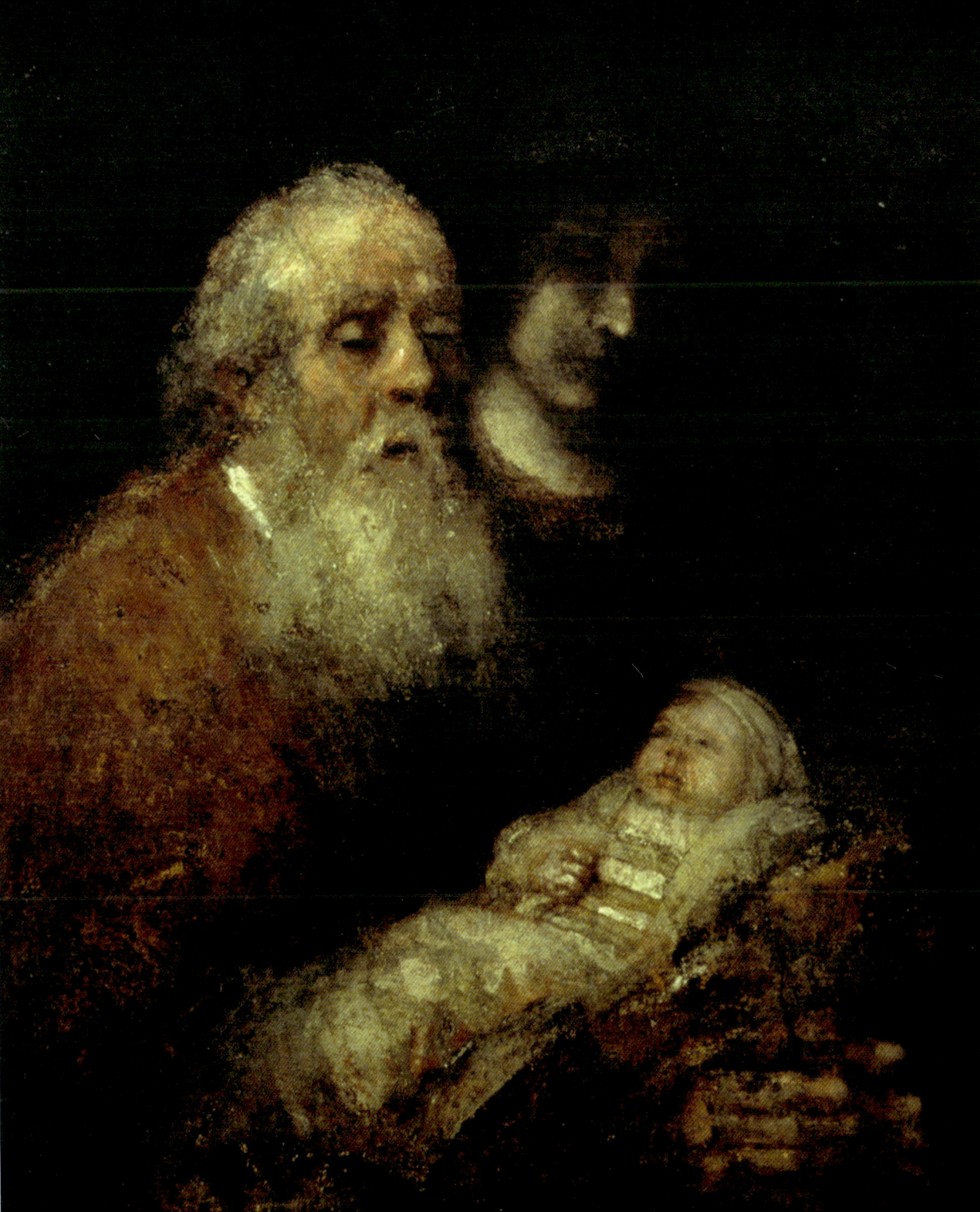

The Rest on the Flight into Egypt (1510)
Gerard David (c. 1455–1523) / National Gallery of Art, Washington, DC, United States

Peace in a Time of Trouble

WHEN HEROD, out of jealousy, wanted to kill the newborn King, he slaughtered all little boys under two years of age. But while Joseph was asleep, an angel in a dream told him to get up in the middle of the night and escape with Jesus and Mary to Egypt.

Though it must have been frightening and hair-raising, here they are so calm and peaceful because they trust in God. Mary is gentle and humble, but also like a queen. The Child has fine golden rays shining from his head. He is a real baby with little toes. Joseph is beating a chestnut tree for food for his family. The donkey is patiently waiting while they rest on their way.

Mary and Jesus look alike. They both have auburn hair. He is flesh of her flesh. Jesus has grapes in His hands, which reminds us of the wine of the Eucharist made from grapes. What does that mean?

It means that the Blood of Jesus Christ, which is the Eucharist, will be shed for love of us. Mary is thinking about this mystery.

> "The fruit of the Spirit is love, joy, peace, patience, kindness, goodness, faithfulness, gentleness, self-control . . ."
>
> —GALATIANS 5:22–23

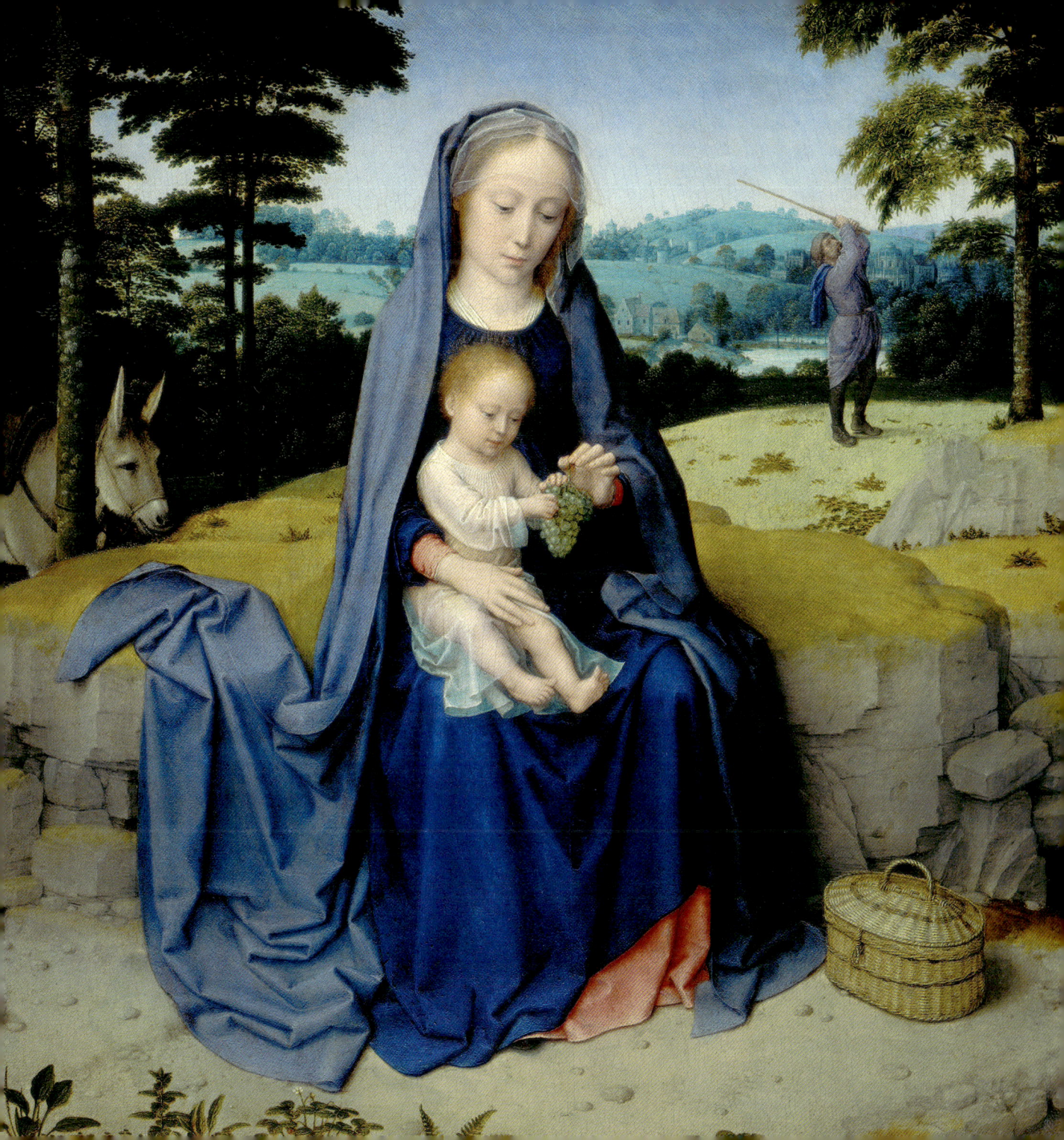

The Angelus (c. 1857–1859)
Jean-François Millet (1814–1875) / Musée D'Orsay, Paris, France

Remembering God while Working

For centuries Christians have been praying what we call the Angelus. The church bell tolls three times a day, morning, noon, and evening, to remind us to pray (in part):

"The Angel of the Lord declared unto Mary, and she conceived of the Holy Spirit. . . . And the Word was made flesh, and dwelt among us."

This helps us remember the most important event in the history of the world. It is a wonderful invention of God's love that God became man and that He is with us in our daily work.

People stop whatever work they are doing to pray the Angelus. These farmers are harvesting potatoes. They have put down their pitchfork and wheelbarrow and are folding their hands while praying. They bow their heads in reverence.

There is a glow of evening twilight, which makes us think of heaven right in the middle of hard labor.

> "May we to whom the Incarnation of Christ . . . was made known by the message of an Angel . . . be brought to the glory of His Resurrection."
>
> —The Angelus

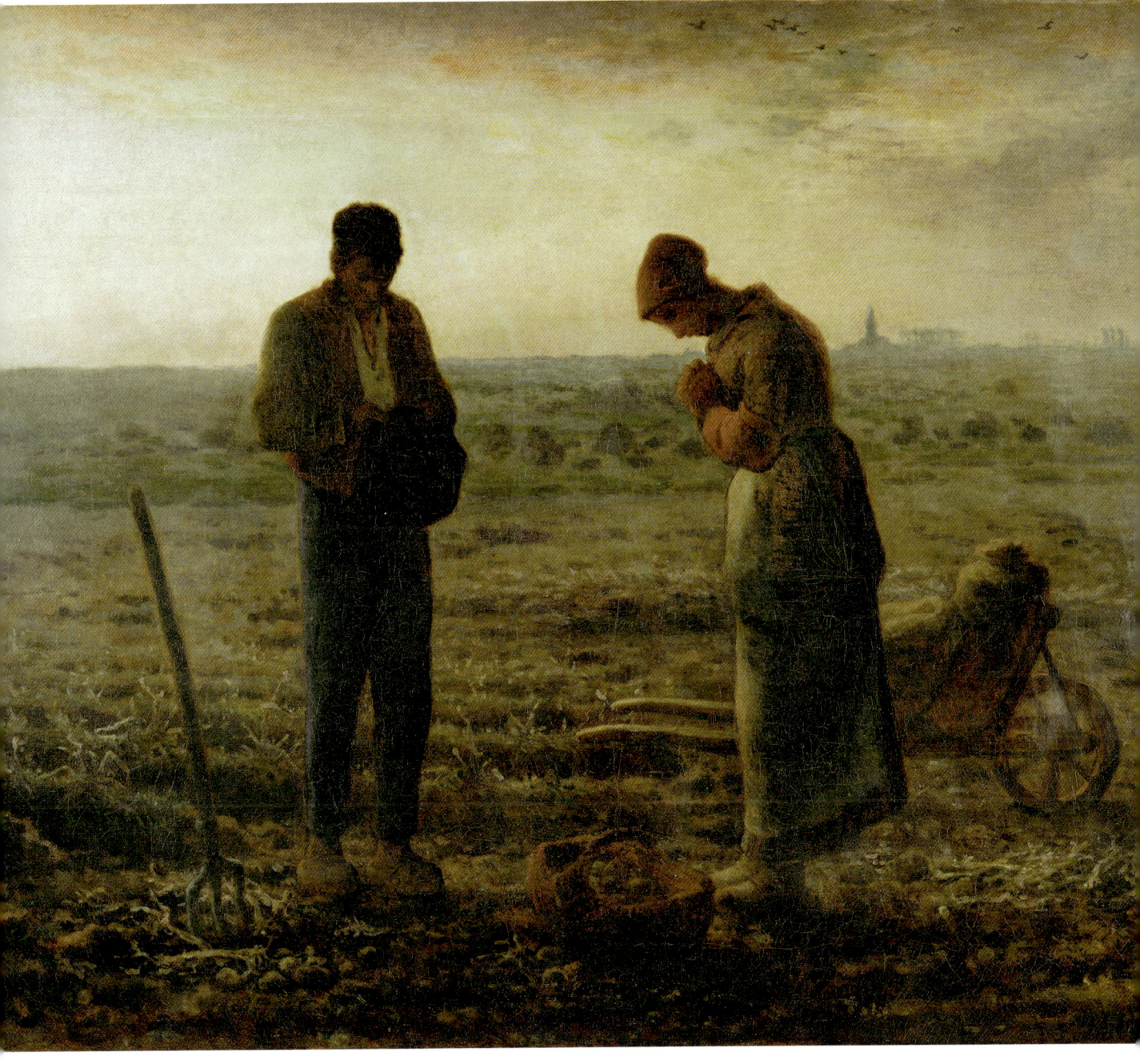

Las Meninas (1656)
Diego Velázquez (1599–1660) / Museo del Prado, Madrid, Spain

The Infanta, Her Family, and Playmates

The Infanta ("Princess" in English) Margarita of Spain is pictured in an artist's studio. The artist who made this painting, Velázquez, has drawn a portrait of himself on the far left. The princess's parents, the powerful King Philip IV and Queen Mariana of Spain, are reflected in the mirror on the back wall. In other words, the Infanta Margarita is looking at her dad and mom.

She is surrounded by her friendly ladies-in-waiting, who are her playmates and also take care of her. In the background are some guards and a nurse.

On the right are two other playmates, a dwarf and a little child having fun with the dog. And even the dog seems to be content.

Everyone is included and part of the family. They are joyful, natural, and at ease.

The Infanta is especially sweet and innocent. The light shines on her. Everyone loves her. God loves each one.

"A little child shall lead them."

—Isaiah 11:6

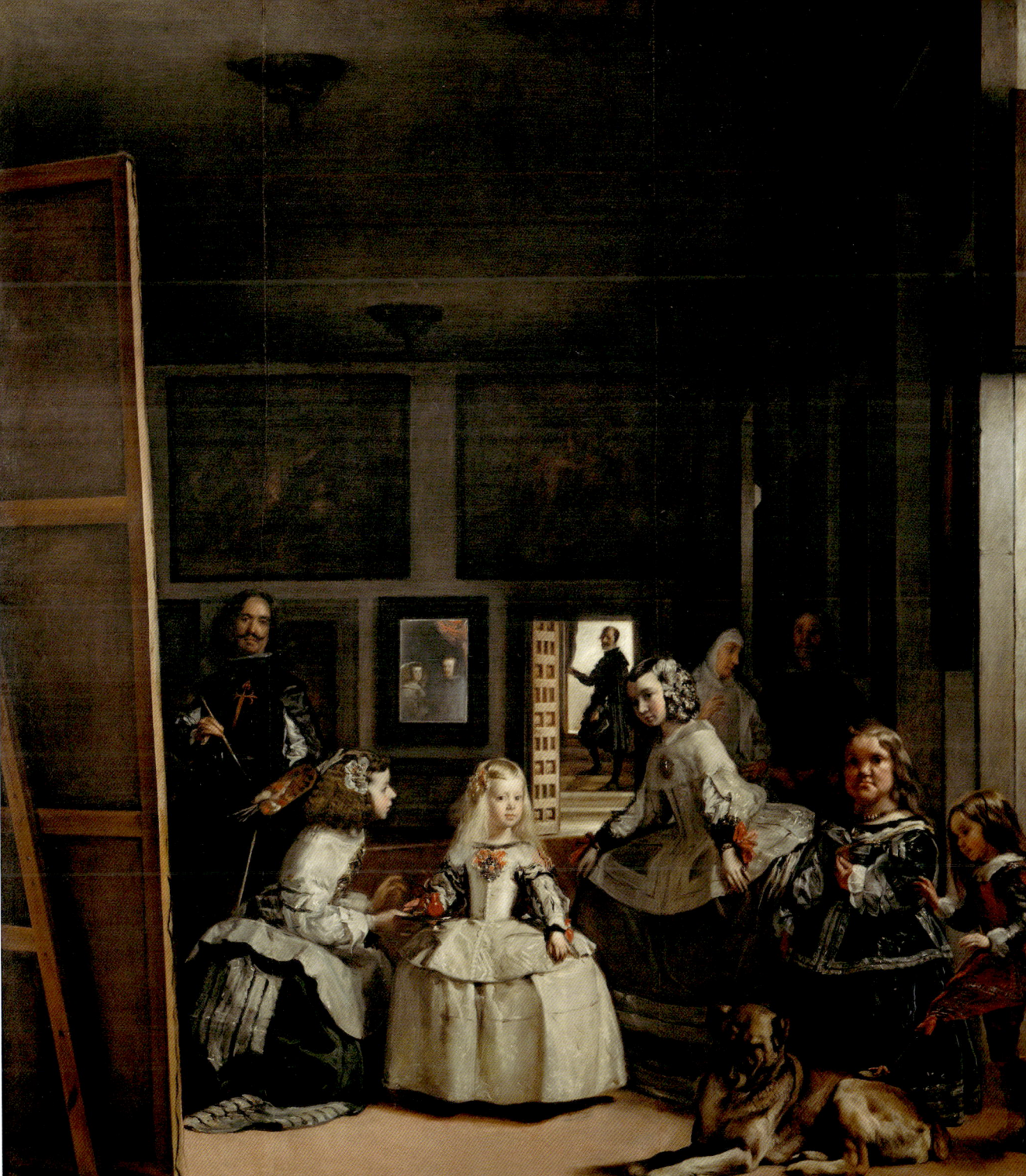

The Old Man and His Grandson (1490)
Domenico Ghirlandaio (1449–1494) / Louvre Museum, Paris France

The Love Between Grandfather and Grandson

This old man with an extraordinary, funny nose has suffered a lot in his long life. It is hard for him to be handicapped like that. Still, he is not angry or bitter or hateful. He is a very kind man and has a wonderful character. He is really good, and people respect him for that.

He accepts the will of God.

He is not thinking of himself, but looks with love at his grandson. His grandson looks up to his grandfather. His little hand reaches up to touch his grandfather, comforting him and showing his affection. He can rely on his grandfather, who is like a rock to him.

The boy is eager to hear all the amazing stories the old man can tell him. And he trusts him. Through a window we see a winding road leading to a mountain. It reminds us of our road in this earthly life on our way to heaven.

"[The Lord] is mindful of us in our affliction, for his mercy endures forever..."

—Psalm 136:23
(From the Douay-Rheims translation.)

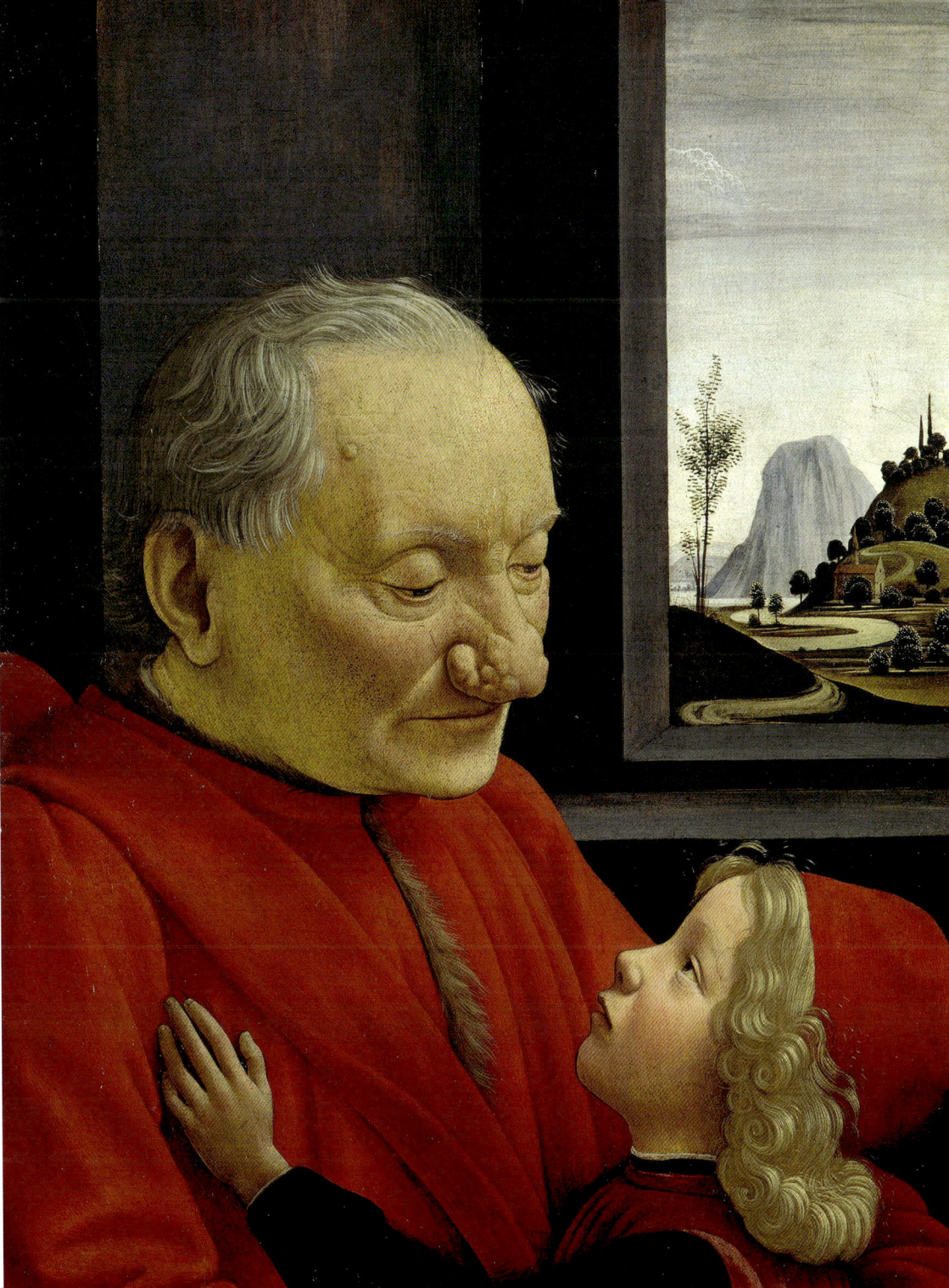

Detail of the Last Judgment (1425–1430)
Fra Angelico (c. 1395–1455) / Museo di San Marco, Florence, Italy

At Heaven's Gate

AFTER DYING, the saints here are about to enter the gate of heaven. Many angels are holding their hands and leading them there.

The saints have fine rays of light coming from their heads. This means that the light of Christ shines through them. The angels have halos, which means they are holy.

No one is lonely or all by him- or herself. They are always surrounded by angels who love them.

We see the grace of God in all of them. They are as graceful as if they were dancing. They are filled with bliss and surpassing joy. The flowers and plants are like jewels.

The two saints about to enter heaven stretch out their arms to meet Jesus. They are flooded with the light of redemption.

> "Without having seen him you love him . . . you believe in him and rejoice with unutterable and exalted joy. As the outcome of your faith you obtain the salvation of your souls."
>
> —1 Peter 1:8–9

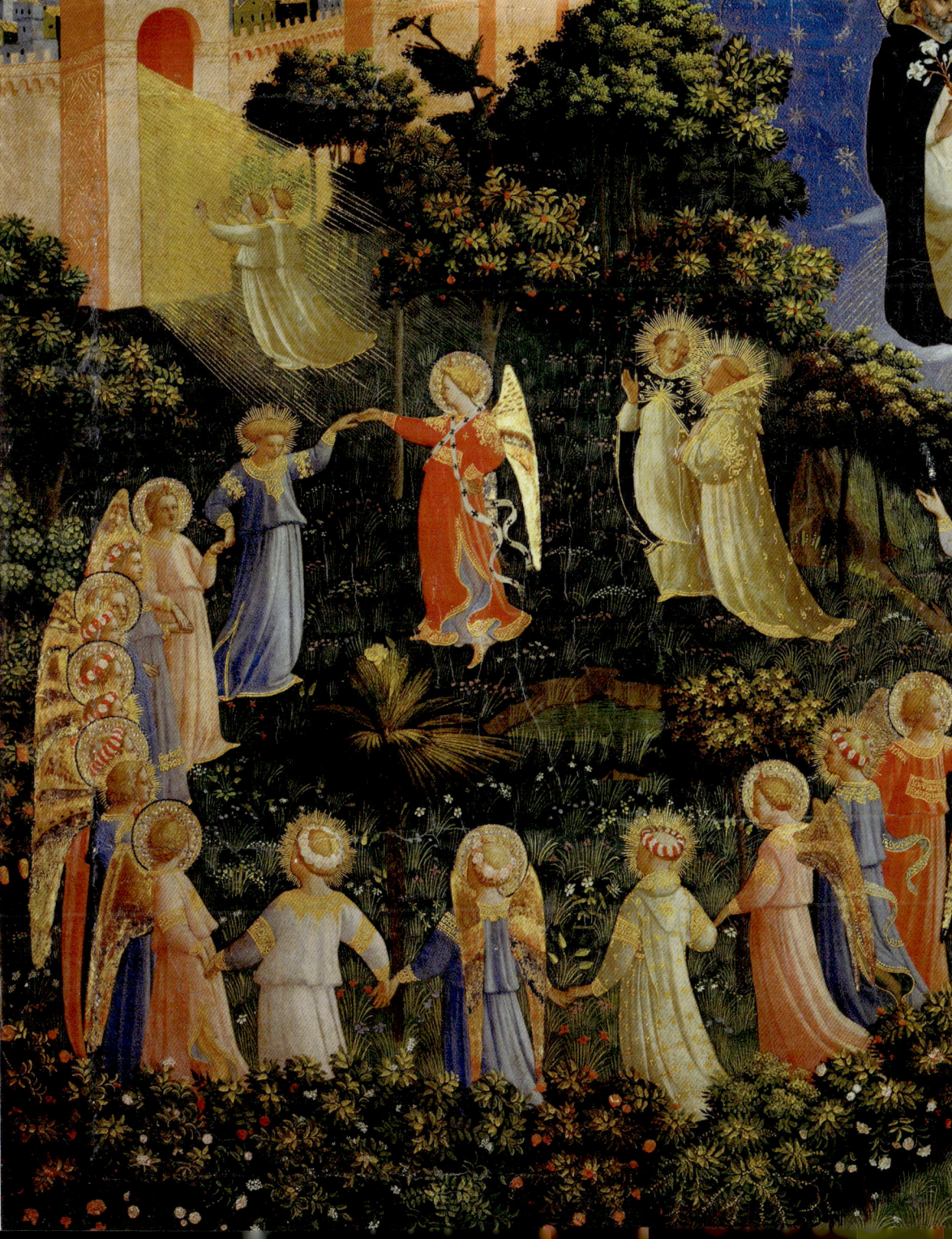

The Little Street (1658)

Johannes Vermeer (c. 1632–1675) / Rijksmuseum, Amsterdam, Netherlands

Peaceful Lives

Here we see people at work and play in their ordinary, everyday lives on a street in the old Dutch town of Delft.

They are not greedily shopping for more and more *stuff*. They are poor and satisfied with the little they have.

The women are doing their daily chores of sweeping, washing, and sewing. They want to make a clean, neat home for their families.

The two children are enchanted by a very plain game on the ground and are having fun. Everything is simple and peaceful.

Do you see the miniature pictures within this picture?

Look at the doorway on the left and see the woman inside working. Now see another doorway on the right with the woman sewing.

These women are doing small deeds of loving care. Everyone is contented and thankful for simple, little things.

"... with all lowliness and meekness, with patience, forbearing one another in love ... in the bond of peace."

—Ephesians 4:2–3

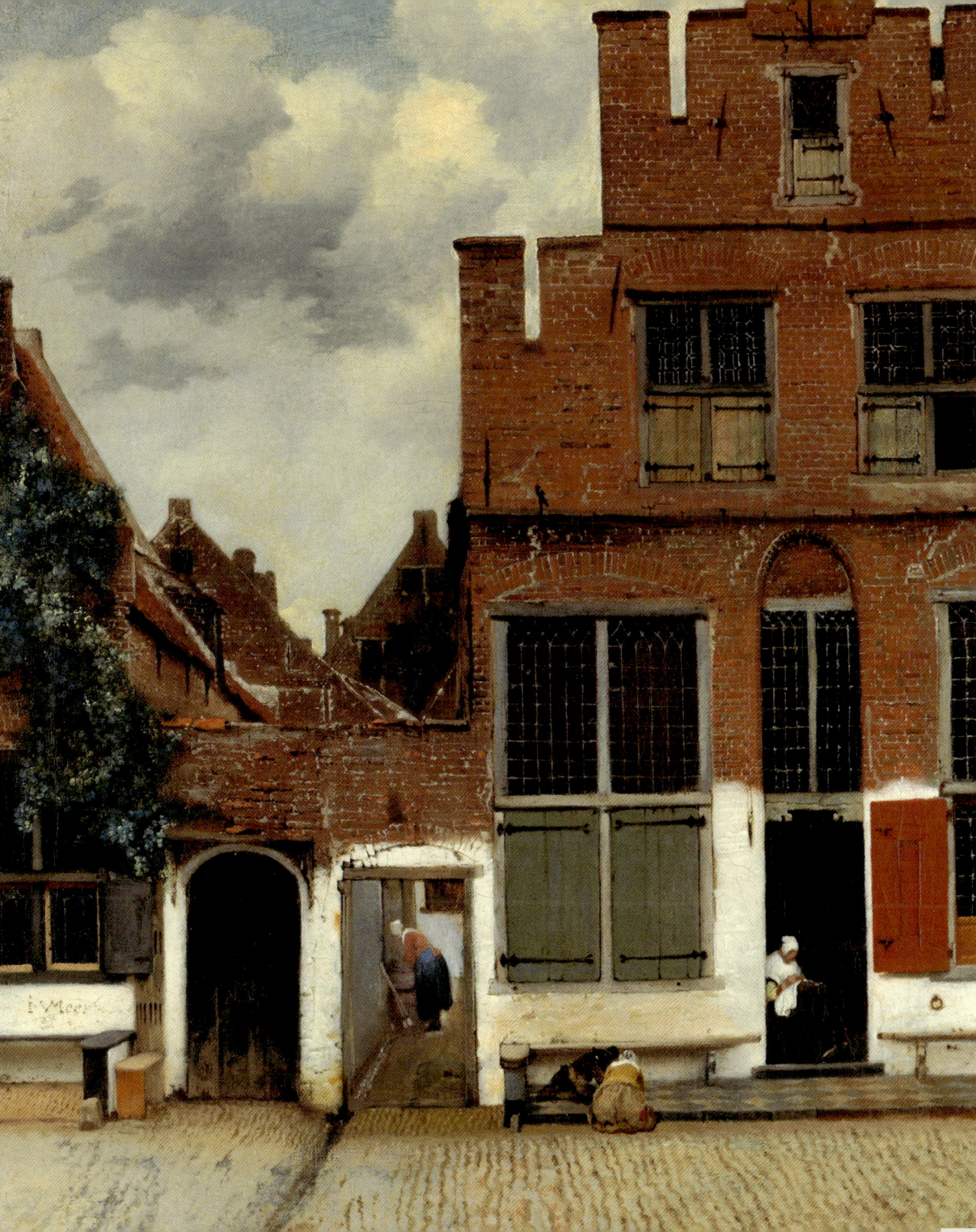

Christ on the Cross Adored by St. Dominic (1440–1445)
Fra Angelico (c. 1395–1455) / Museo di San Marco, Florence, Italy

Love for Love without End

WHEN CHRIST WAS DYING on the Cross, Mary, St. John, Mary Magdalene, and some women were with Him. However, here St. Dominic, who lived centuries later, is kneeling at the Crucifixion.

What do you think the artist, Fra Angelico, means? He is showing how everyone is invited to kneel at the foot of the Cross with Jesus to love and adore Him.

At the very moment when the lambs for the Jewish Passover are offered, Jesus, the true Lamb of God, pours out His blood to save us from our sins.

As He dies, Jesus is looking down at St. Dominic with infinite love. St. Dominic, with his arms hugging the Cross, is looking up with burning love.

This love between Jesus and us is without measure. It is how we pray with trust. And it is an unbreakable bond with God.

> "Greater love has no man than this, that a man lay down his life for his friends."
>
> —JOHN 15:13

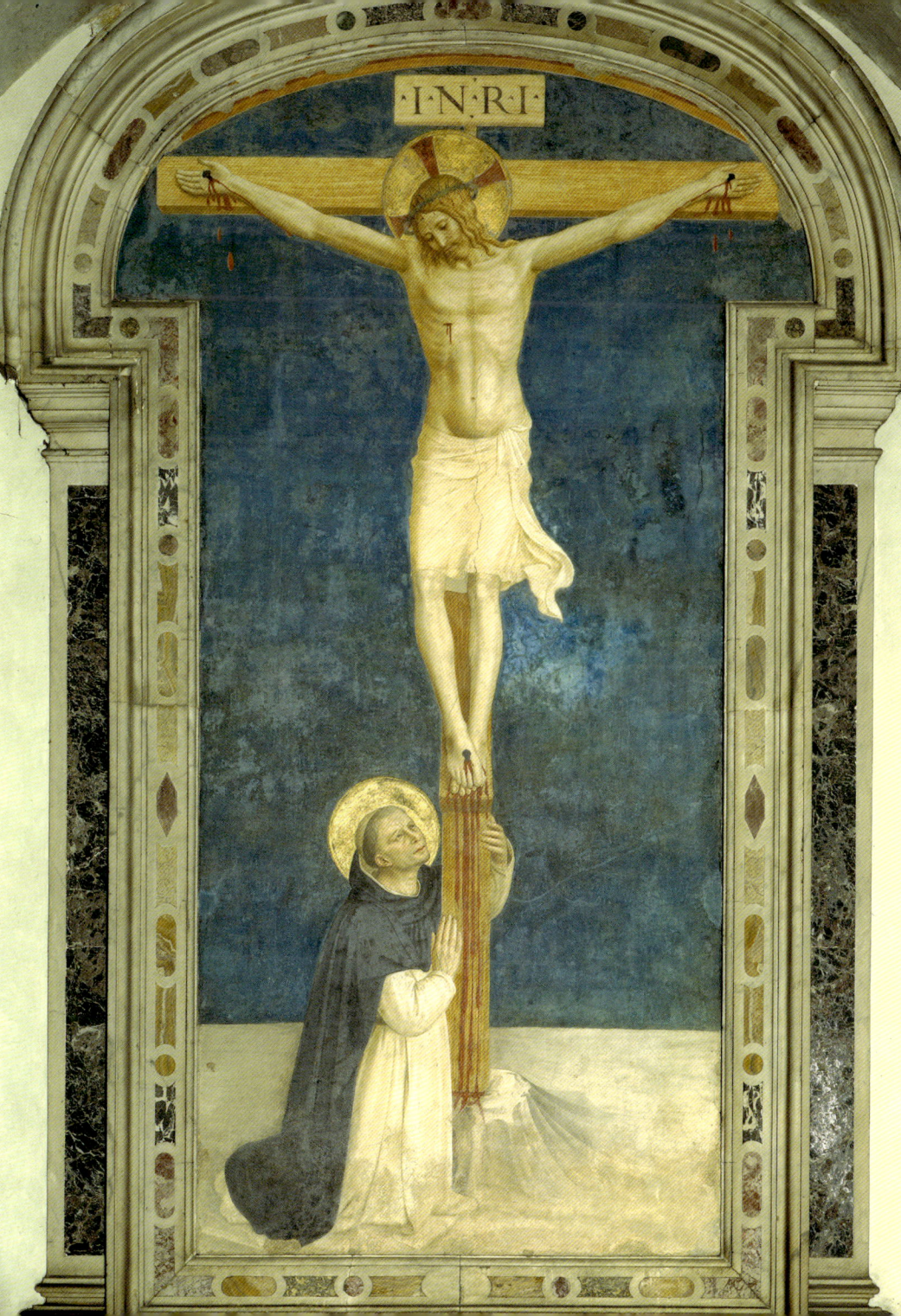

The Adoration of the Shepherds (1485)
Domenico Ghirlandaio (1449–1494) / Sassetti Chapel, Basilica Santa Trinità, Florence, Italy

The Most Beautiful Thing that Ever Happened

This is a painting of the most beautiful thing that ever happened. It is the birth of Jesus. God became man, an infant on the ground.

The shepherds are the first to come to adore Jesus. The one in brown is a self-portrait of Ghirlandaio, the artist.

Even the animals seem amazed. St. Joseph is looking up at the angel. A large crowd in bright colors with horses are all running to see what has happened. Everyone feels great joy. Their hearts are singing. The city of Jerusalem is in the landscape.

Mary the mother of Jesus has her mantle spread under Him. With her head tenderly bent over Him and her hands in adoration, she is inviting everyone to adore Him.

Because of that she is the most beautiful, most lovely, and most holy of all women. She is full of grace.

> "O fairest among women . . .
> Your cheeks are comely with ornaments . . .
> You are all fair, my love; there is no flaw in you."
>
> —Song of Songs 1:8–9; 4:7

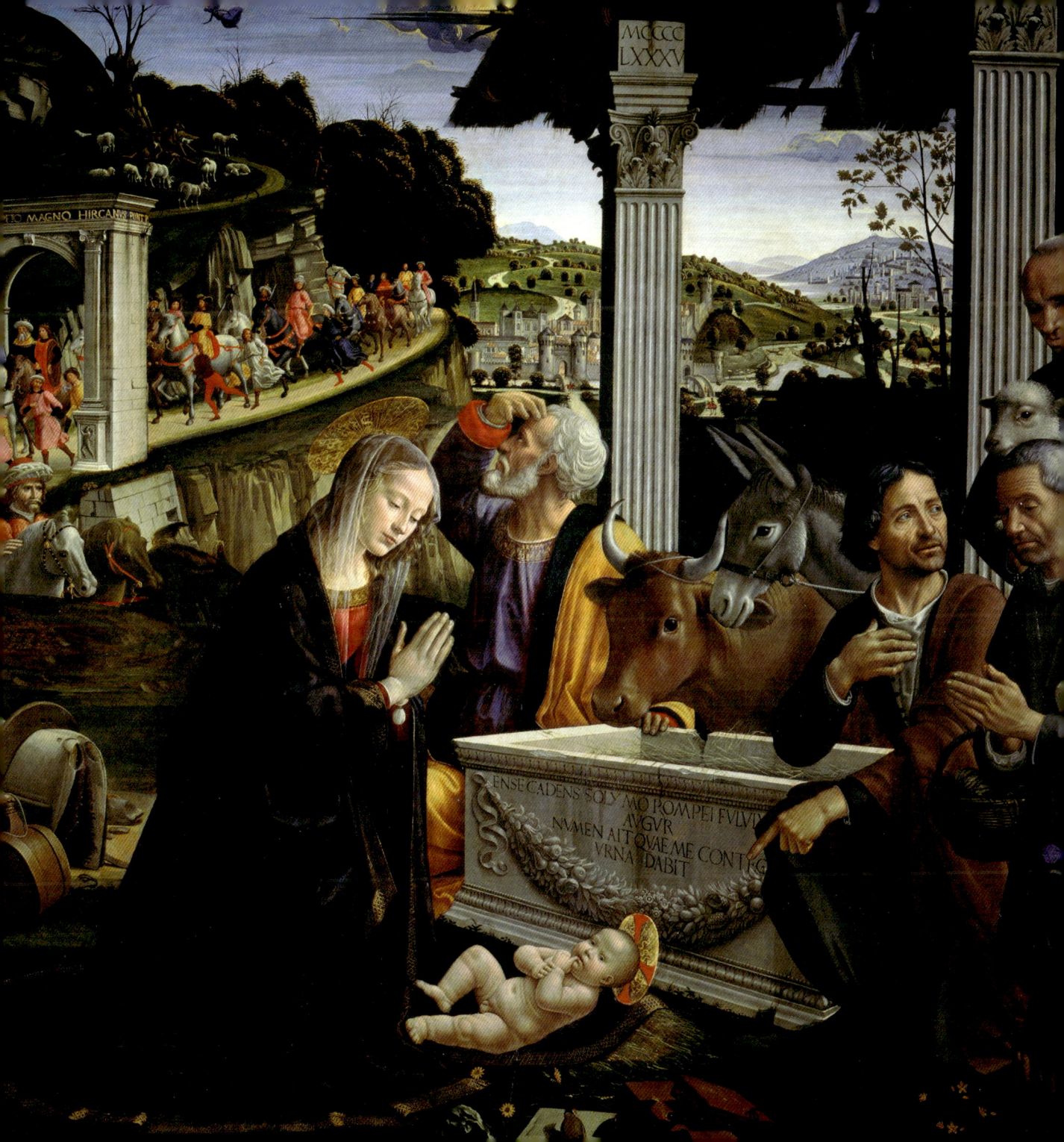

St. Francis in the Desert (c.1480)
Giovanni Bellini (c.1424/36–1516) / The Frick Museum, New York, United States

Enchanted by God's Beauty

St. Francis of Assisi often went into the mountains and desert to pray.
He loved Jesus so much and saw all people as his brothers and sisters—and animals, birds, and fish as well, because God made them all. He asked them all to praise God for His goodness. He thanked God for having made all these wonderful creatures.

Every plant, tree, and twig is precious in this painting. The donkey is humble. On the left is a heron.

On the desk is a Bible. The city, the distant hills, and the sky are radiant.

St. Francis is looking toward a great shining light. The rocks reflect this light. His arms are open and and stretched out in astonishment at this beauty. He is seeing a vision of Jesus in glory.

He is receiving the sacred wounds of Christ, called the stigmata, in his body.

St. Francis is filled with awe, wonder, and thanksgiving.

> "Praised be Thou my Lord for Brother Sun . . . he is beautiful and radiant with great splendor . . . for Sister Moon and the stars. . . ."
>
> —St. Francis of Assisi, "Canticle of the Sun"

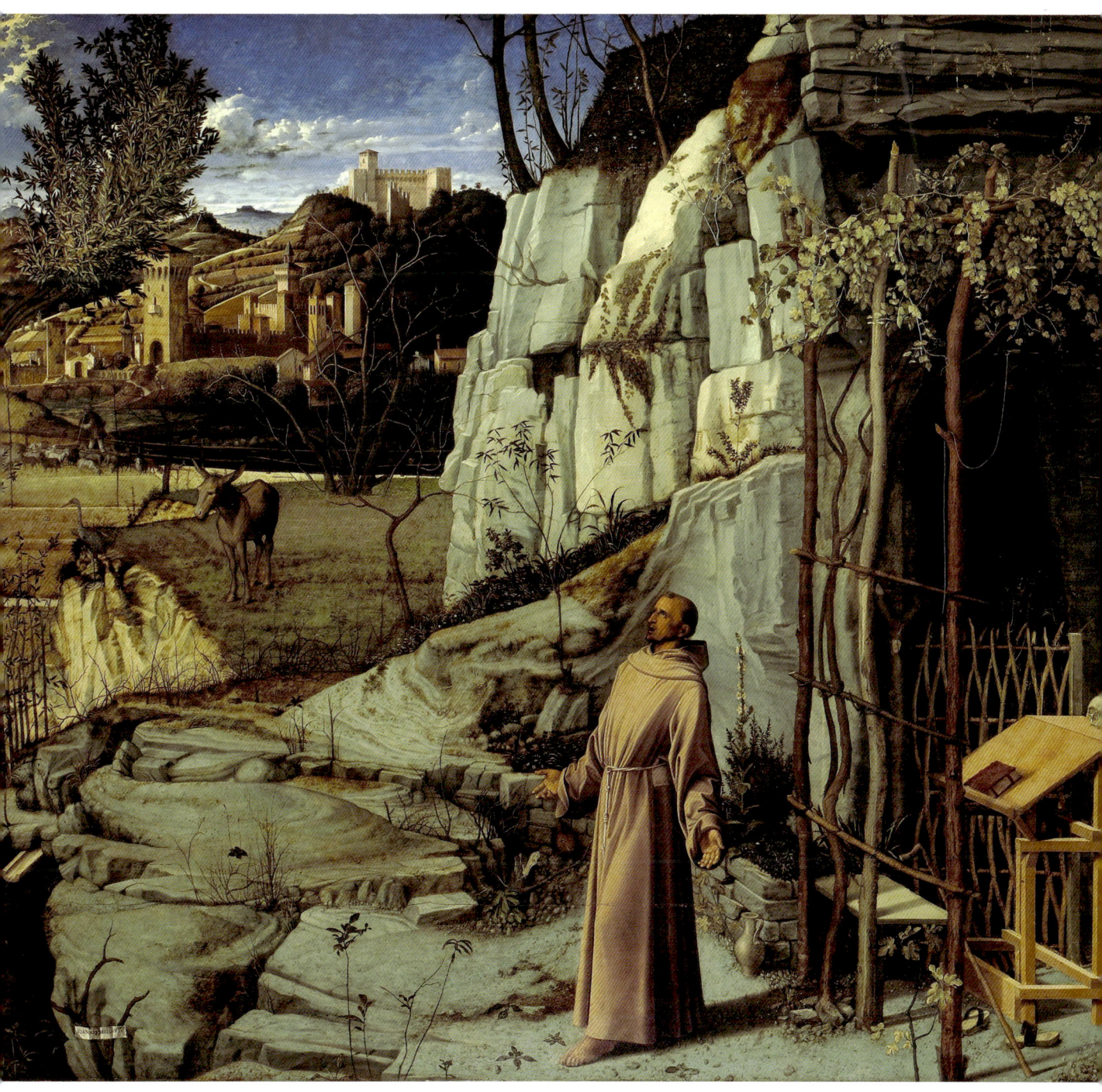

Dad's Coming (1873)
Winslow Homer (1836–1910) / National Gallery of Art, Washington, D.C., United States

Waiting

MORE THAN ONE HUNDRED YEARS ago fierce storms raged in the ocean near Massachusetts. Many fishermen went far out with huge nets to do deep sea fishing. Some were shipwrecked and lost their lives.

This picture was painted soon after that time. This family is patiently waiting for their dad.

The sea is now peaceful. The boy is perched high on a boat like a lookout eagerly waiting for his dad. Like his dad, he loves adventure.

However, the mother is clinging to her little girl. She is a bit afraid and anxious. Still, she is quiet, and realizes that God's loving care is alive.

The sailboats give hope. The sea is so beautiful. It reminds her of God's almighty power. God alone is in charge and has control. This family's trust is in God, our Father, who always has loving plans for us.

> "Let not your hearts be troubled, neither let them be afraid. . . . I am with you always . . ."
>
> —JOHN 14:27, MATTHEW 28:20

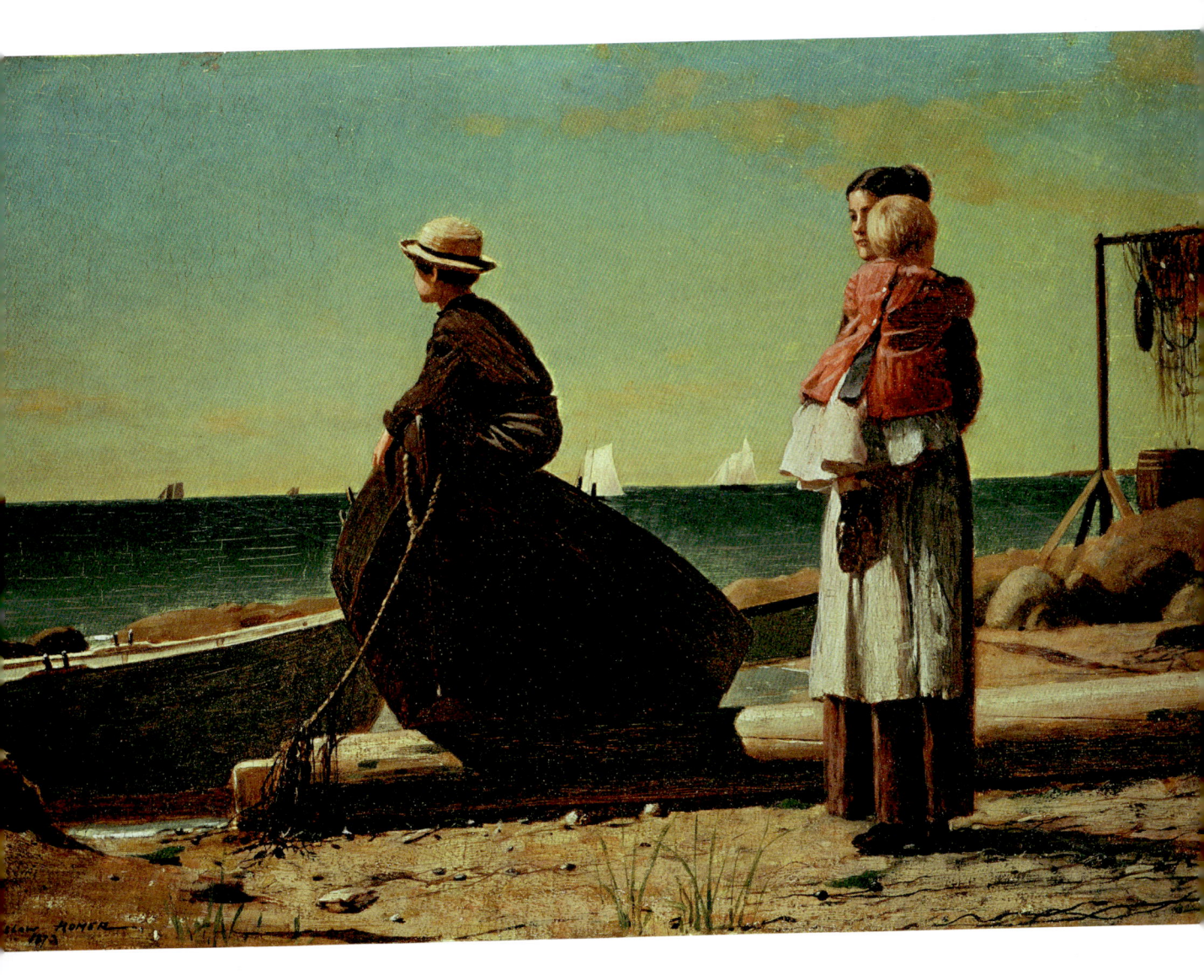

The Three Archangels with Tobias (c. 1470)
Francesco Botticini (c. 1446–1498) / Uffizi Gallery, Florence, Italy

Guardians by Our Side

ARCHANGELS ARE mysterious beings. They are the most powerful angels. The Archangel Raphael is holding the hand of young Tobias to bring him and his little dog home to Tobit, his father. They are carrying a fish and a jar of fish oil in Raphael's hand to cure Tobit's blindness.

On the right is the Archangel Gabriel. He will soon invite Mary to become the mother of Jesus.

On the left is the Archangel Michael, who fights the devil with his sword. He wears armor so that the devil cannot pierce through.

Though angels are invisible spirits, they are very real. Sometimes they appear in human form. They are extremely beautiful.

Angels take care of us and are always near us. They are also continually in God's Presence. They bring us closer to God.

> Angels appeared to Zechariah in Luke 1:11–20 and to Mary in Luke 1:26–38. An angel appeared at Fatima in 1916. Can you think of other times when angels have appeared? What was their message?

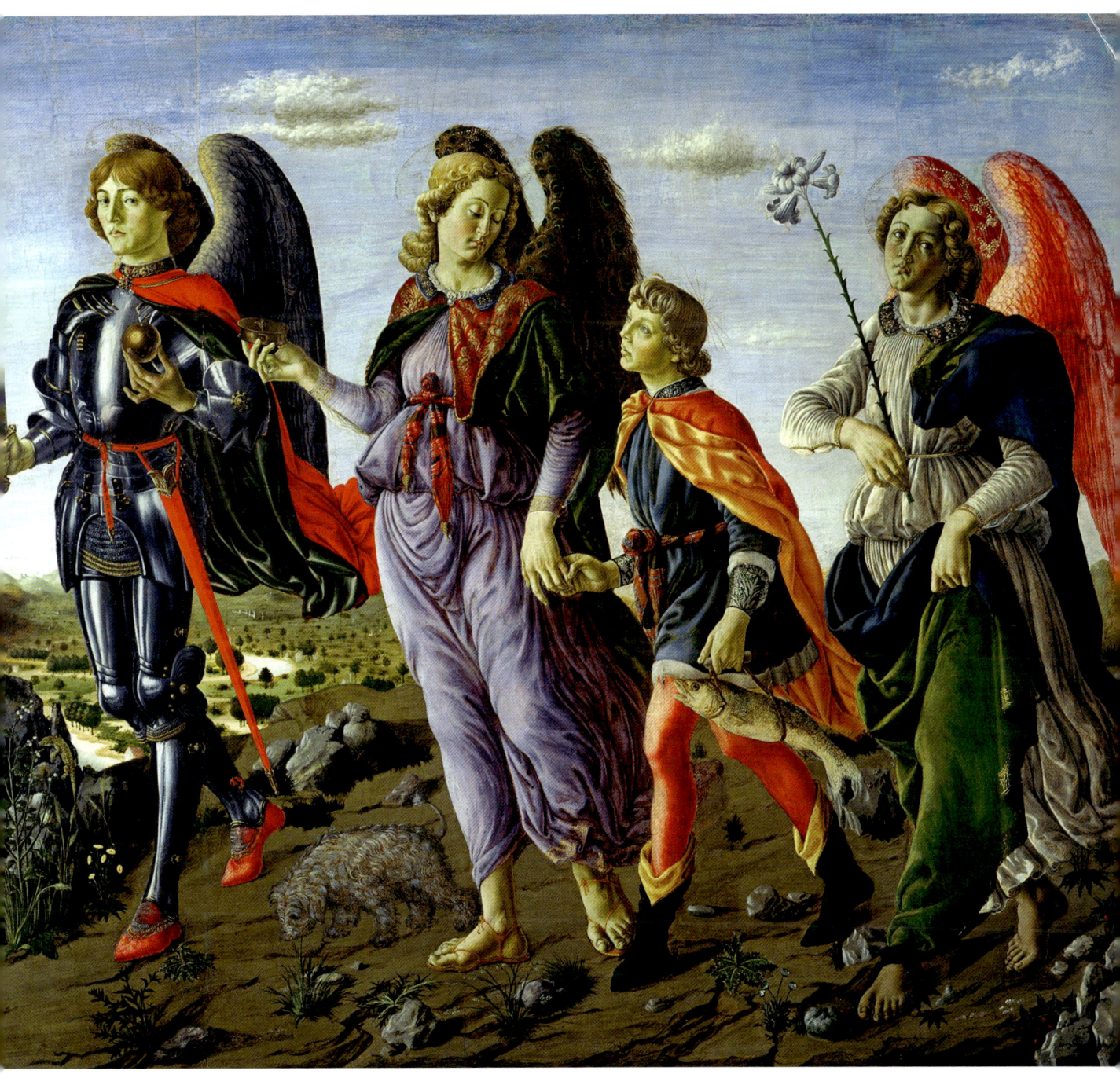

Thomas More (1527)
Hans Holbein (1497–1543) / The Frick Museum, New York, United States

A Man of Courage

Thomas More was Lord Chancellor of England under King Henry VIII almost five hundred years ago.

When King Henry left his wife Queen Catherine and wanted to marry Anne Boleyn, Thomas refused his consent because doing this was against God's commandment. When the King made himself the head of the Church, Thomas would not agree.

The portrait shows that Thomas is a man of honesty, with a strong but peaceful character.

His eyes look straight forward and upwards toward higher things of heaven and the eternal law. He knew that what the king wanted was bad. Thomas loved God above all else. It took great courage to follow his conscience and stand up to the king. He knew it meant death.

The king had him beheaded. He died as a martyr for his faith. St. Thomas More is now known as one of the great saints of England and of the whole world.

St. Thomas More said: "I die the king's good servant, but God's first."

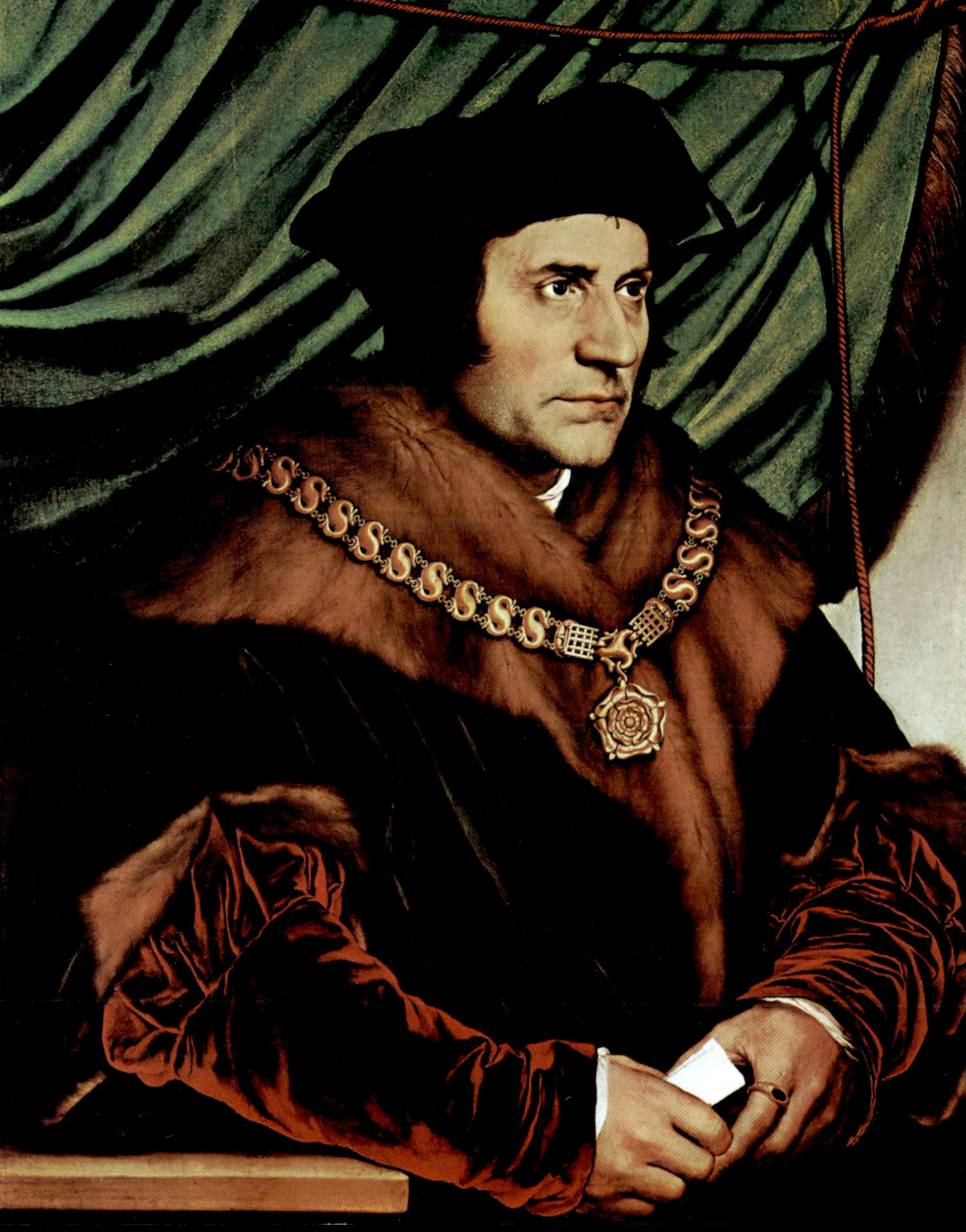

St. Paul's Conversion on the Way to Damascus (1601)
Michelangelo Merisi da Caravaggio (1571–1610) / Santa Maria del Popolo, Rome

The Power of God's Grace

Saul (later called Paul) was on his way to Damascus to slaughter the disciples of Christ. Suddenly a light from heaven shone around him.

A voice called, "Saul, Saul, why do you persecute me?" Saul was actually persecuting Christ when he persecuted Christ's disciples.

Here St. Paul is knocked off his horse, shattered, humbled, prostrate on the ground, his sword thrown down.

Why is he in this odd upside down position? It was because he needed to change his life completely since he had been so proud.

The light in the dark over him is mysterious and beautiful. He is stretching his arms toward Jesus in a rapture of love and in helplessness toward his Savior.

St. Paul was instantly struck blind, for a time, because he had to learn to see with the eyes of faith.

This was a miracle of God's grace. It changed the history of Christianity.

> "[Nothing] in all creation will be able to separate us from the love of God in Christ Jesus Our Lord."
>
> —Romans 8:39

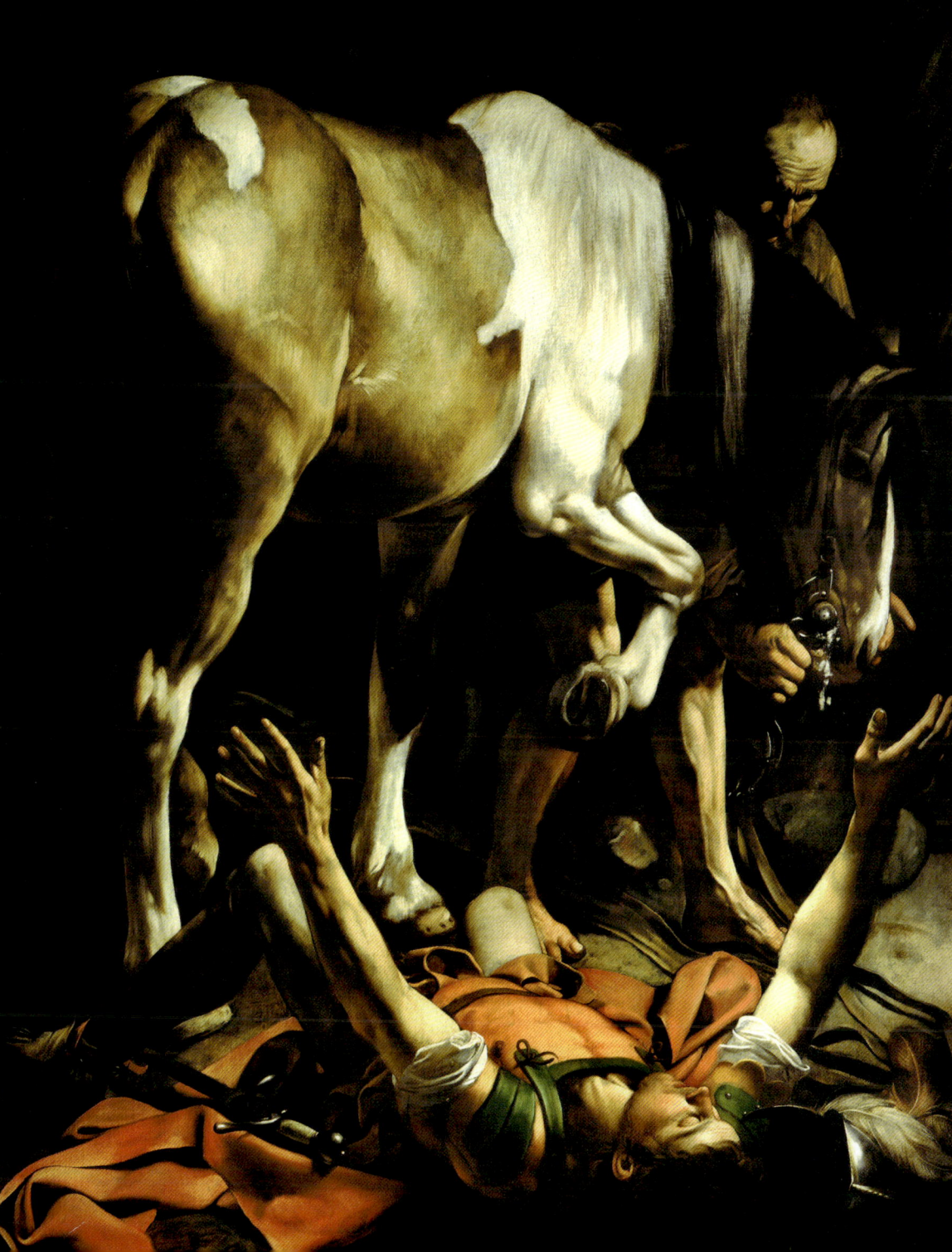

Detail of Joachim and Anne at the Golden Gate of Jerusalem (1304–1306)
Giotto di Bondone (c. 1266/7–1337) / Scrovengi Chapel, Padua, Italy

---

Married Love

These two paintings are all about the true beauty of selfless married love.

THE FIRST IS the story of Joachim and Anne, the parents of the Blessed Virgin Mary. For many years they prayed for a child.

Finally, they learned they were expecting a baby. They were so filled with joy over this gift of God that they ran to hug each other out of sheer happiness.

Joachim and Anne are so closely united that their two faces look like one face, with two eyes, one nose, and lips. Their hands are tender and loving.

It is as if God is there with them, uniting them as one family with the unborn child in their midst.

> "A man shall . . . be joined to his wife, and the two shall become one flesh."
>
> —EPHESIANS 5:31

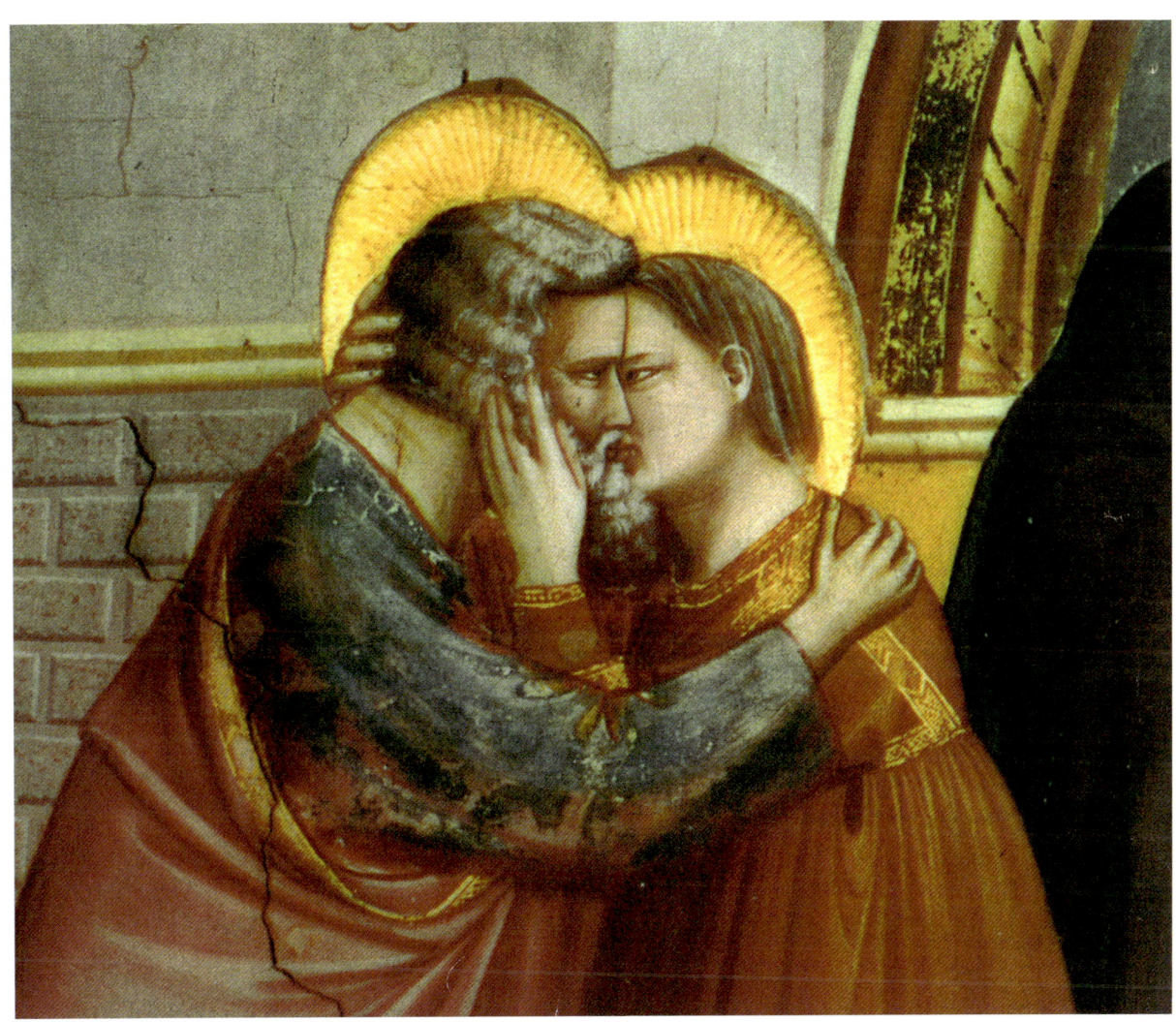

The Jewish Bride (c. 1665–1669)
Rembrandt Harmenszoon van Rijn (c. 1606–1669) Rijksmuseum, Amsterdam, Netherlands

T HE SECOND PICTURE IS of a bridegroom and bride. He is bending slightly in order to protect her. He is respectful. His hand on her is reverent, trusting, and loving. He cherishes her like a precious treasure. She is blushing a little bit. She is glowing.

She trusts him completely. Her fingers gently touch his with tender love. The artist shows the love of her heart by the scarlet red of her dress. It tells us that she will be like a warm fire in the hearth of their home.

The man and woman are giving themselves to each other for life.

"Love is the sweet and holy bond that binds the soul with her Creator; it binds God in man and man in God."

—ST. CATHERINE OF SIENA

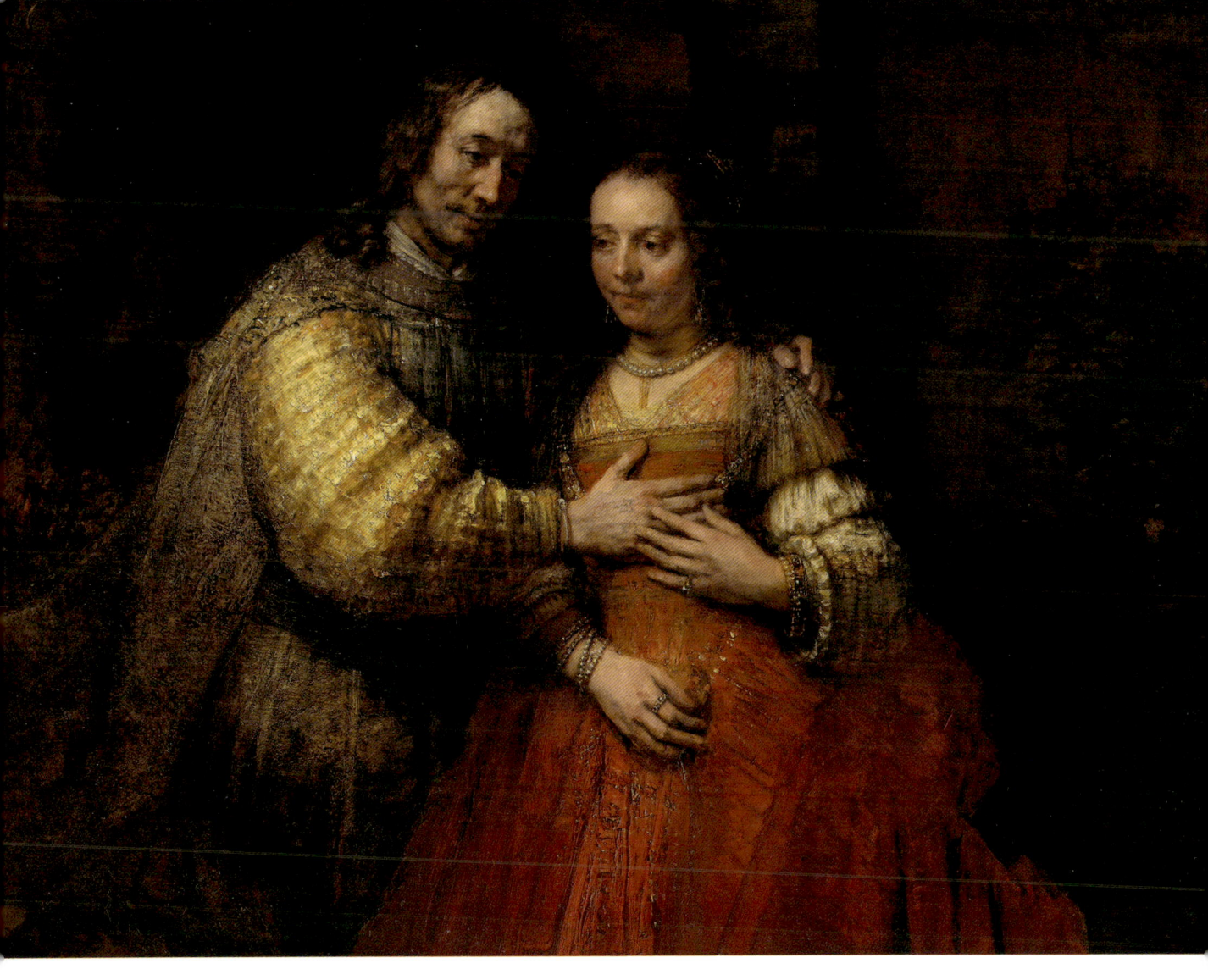

The Surrender at Breda (1634/5)
Diego Velázquez (1599–1660) / Museo del Prado, Madrid, Spain

After the Fighting

The battle at Breda in the Netherlands between the Dutch and Spanish armies has just ended. In the background the fires on the wide battlefields are still burning. It must have been fierce and bloody.

Then something thrilling happens. Enemies are reconciled. On the left the defeated Dutch forces are in a bit of disarray. On the right the victorious Spaniards stand with their spears in near perfect order.

The former two opponents, Justinus the Dutch governor and Spinola the general of the Spaniards, are meeting. Justinus is handing over the key to the city of Breda. Spinola has just descended from his beautiful, powerful horse in front. He could have remained proudly on his horse, but he didn't. He is gently bending forward, extending his arm with his hand on his former enemy's shoulder.

It shows great kindness and true forgiveness. He also seems to praise Justinus for his bravery. Justinus is bowing with trust, goodwill, and respect.

This picture is about the victory of Christian forgiveness, and of generous love between former rivals.

> "If you forgive men their trespasses, your heavenly Father also will forgive you..."
>
> —Matthew 6:14

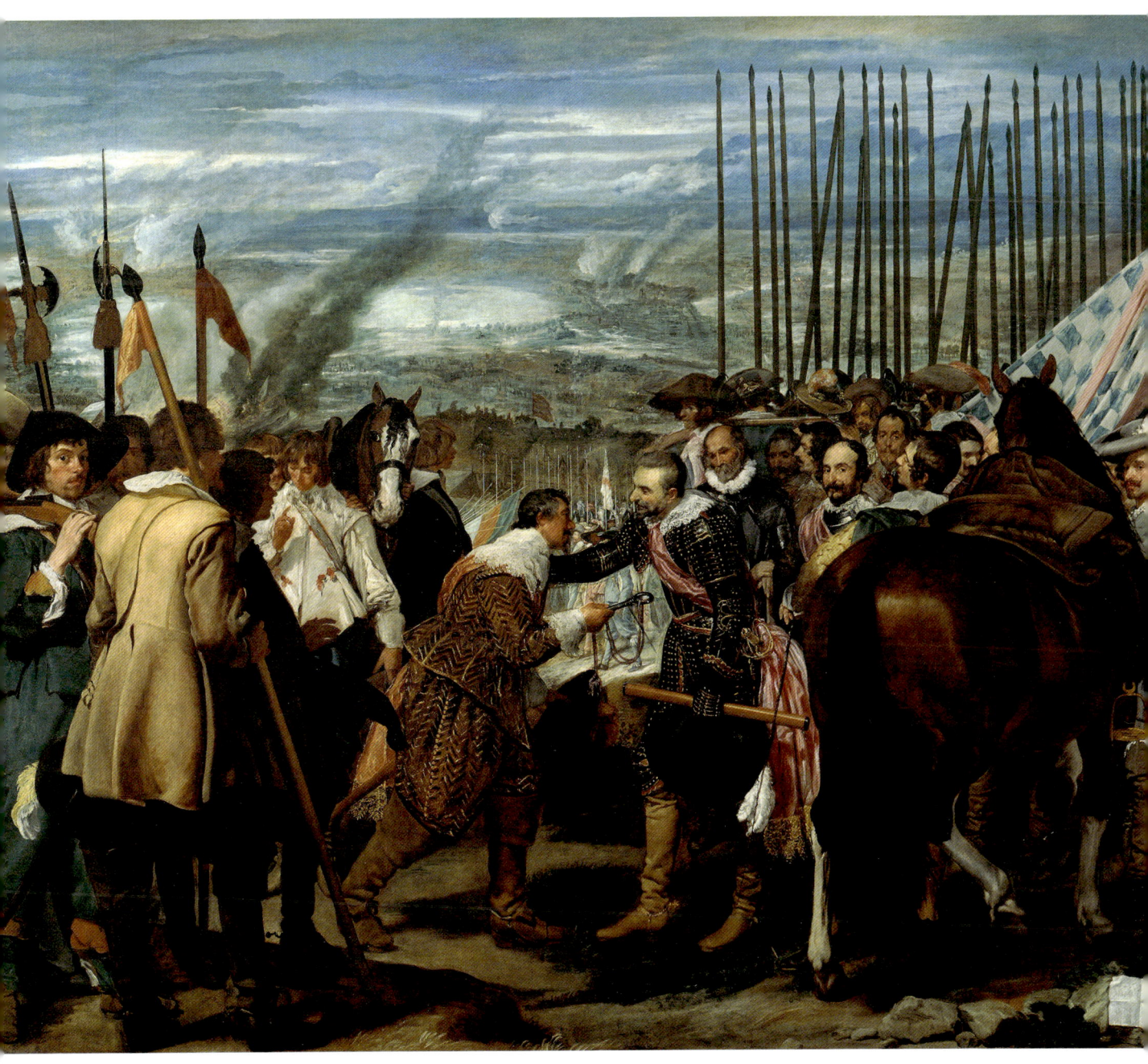

The Resurrection (c. 1463–1465)
Piero della Francesca (c. 1415–1492) / Civic Museum in San Sepolcro, Tuscany, Italy

The Miracle of Christ's Resurrection

Some pictures of the Risen Christ show Him more like an unearthly angel. However, here He is the King of kings and Lord of lords, alive in glorious majesty.

The guards are still asleep. In the background on the left we see leafless trees, and on the right they are blooming. What do you think that means? It shows us the world before and after Christ's Resurrection.

Just hours ago Jesus was suffering, crushed, and dead. Suddenly He rises, with His muscular foot on the tomb like a powerful athlete, surging upwards from the grave. It is the greatest miracle.

His garment is a rose color, the color of joy. He is the victorious King holding high the banner of the Cross. The sacred wounds are visible in His body.

A shining halo crowns His head. His eyes are penetrating and all-seeing. His face is all-knowing, awe-inspiring, and holy.

He is divine.

"The Lord has risen indeed…"

—Luke 24:34

Alleluia!

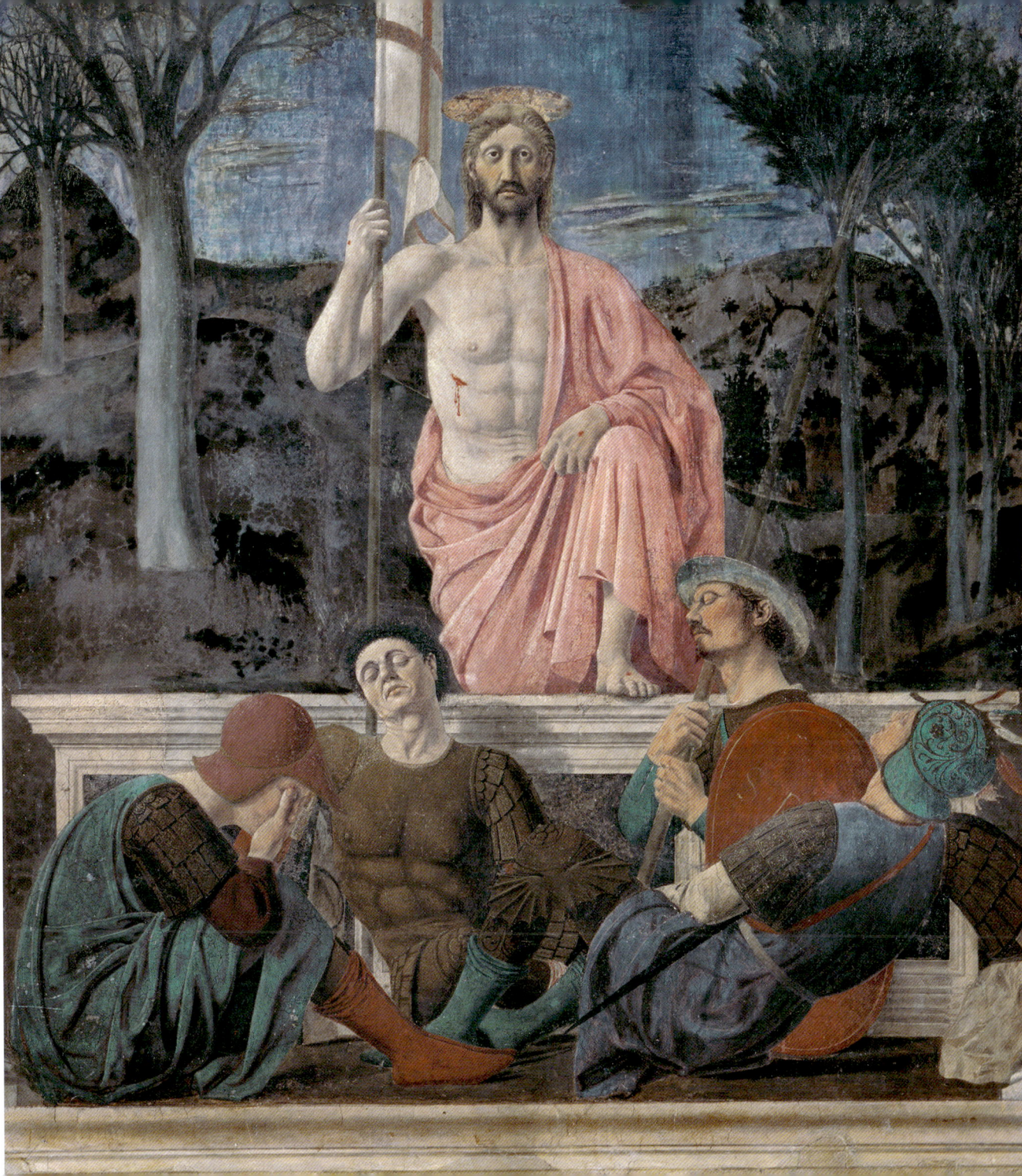

Image Attributions

Simeon with the Christ Child in the Temple / Rembrandt Harmenszoon van Rijn: Kavaler / Art Resource, NY

The Angelus / Jean-François Millet: Erich Lessing / Art Resource, NY

Detail of the Last Judgement / Fra Angelico: Erich Lessing / Art Resource, NY

Christ on the Cross Adored by St. Dominic / Fra Angelico: Nimatallah / Art Resource, NY

The Adoration of the Shepherds / Domenico Ghirlandaio: Scala / Art Resource, NY

The Resurrection / Piero della Francesca: Scala / Art Resource, NY